Lord, Teach Me How to PRAY

by

Dr. Pattie Pendry

Lord, Teach Me How to Pray
Copyright © 1998 by Pattie Pendry
ALL RIGHTS RESERVED

All Scripture references are from the Authorized King James Version of the Bible, unless otherwise marked.

Published by:

Serenity Books
P.O. Box 3595
Hagerstown, MD 21742

ISBN 1-884369-88-X

Printed in the United States of America
For Worldwide Distribution

DEDICATION

To Mary Elizabeth and Bill Eakes, who have always been there for me.

Acknowledgments

First of all, I want to thank my Heavenly Father, and Jesus my Savior for giving me the strength and knowledge to write this book.

Special thanks are due also:

To Carole Kottyan, who is very special and has a great call in life.

To my husband Michael, and children Keith, Patrick, and Elizabeth, who have all been very patient with me as I write long hours into the early morning.

To my sister in the Lord Patricia Sparrow, who has compiled much work for me.

To my dear Grandmother Susie Alston who is now ninety-seven years old and has taught me so much through her wisdom.

To Joseph Earl, who is so humble and kind.

To Leah Everette, for typing my poems.

Hey Gang, I love you all! Thanks!

ABOUT THE POET AND AUTHOR

Dr. Pattie Pendry is a writer, poet, who gives the Lord credit for her success. She is married (she and her husband minister together quite often), a mother of three children, and is a minister of the Gospel.

Dr. Pendry, a lady who really loves the Lord, has a vision for the world and really practices what she preaches. This vision has taken her to Haiti, the Dominican Republic, Israel, Jordan, Egypt, Germany, Austria, Russia, and many other places abroad, and also in the United States. Overseas, she has taken Bibles, food, clothes, medicine, and, most of all, the love of Jesus.

She is an inspired writer, poet, minister, and counselor. She has prayed with and met many movie and television actors and actresses.

She has also appeared on television programs, such as BUYING POWER, and has been a guest of several radio talk shows. Dr. Pendry produced her own television program called THE JOY OF LOVE. She has hosted many exchange students, and was the director of the Students Clothes Closet, where she gave college students free clothes and free counseling.

Dr. Pendry loves people and truly loves the Lord.

She has also received many plaques and awards, and she gives God all the glory.

She has written several tracts, and is the author of many books. She is a speaker and teacher, and conducts motivational workshops. Her poems are very encouraging and uplifting.

Dr. Pendry has a special ministry to professionals and has talked to and prayed with congressmen and other political figures. She has dined with the Ambassador from Lebanon's wife and met with the Ambassador from Finland. Recently, she met with a town councilman who invited her to meet with the town's mayor. These types of meetings have given Dr. Pendry the opportunity to encourage people in leadership with prayer and to let them know that the world needs Jesus.

Dr. Pendry prays that her poems will spread love to your heart. She has listened to many people in her life and wiped away many of their tears. She wants others to know that there is always hope.

> *"Happiness is not making a million dollars. Happiness is sharing, listening and reaching out to others. I want to be that bridge over troubled waters — to bridge the gap for people of all nations to come together in love."*

Be blessed as you read Dr. Pendry's book and poems.

Wherefore also we pray always for you, that our God would count you worthy of this calling, and fulfil all the good pleasure of his goodness, and the work of faith with power: That the name of our Lord Jesus Christ may be glorified in you, and ye in him, according to the grace of our God and the Lord Jesus Christ.

2 Thessalonians 1:11-12

CONTENTS

Introduction 10

1. Did Jesus Pray? 12
2. Jesus Teaches His Disciples How to Pray 18
3. My Experience In Prayer 23
4. Ten Men and Women Who Prayed and Got
   Results 29
5. Sample Prayers and God's Promised
   Answer 40
6. My Prayer for Anorexics and Bulimics 72
7. My Prayer for Pastors 78
8. My Prayer for Politicians 83
9. A Prayer of Repentance 88

Poems by Dr. Pattie Pendry 92
   Strength 93
   Praise Me, Saith the Lord 94
   Give Thanks 95
   God's in Control 97
   The Shepherd That Led My Sheep Astray 98
   His Love 99
   Life Holds This Moment 100
   We Make the Difference 102
   Hope 103
   God's Creation 104
   Life Without Rain 105
   The Hand 106
   God Will See You Through 107
   The Lonely Tree 108
   God is Awesome 110
   Let's Come Together 111

One of his disciples said unto him, LORD, TEACH US TO PRAY, as John also taught his disciples. Luke 11:1

INTRODUCTION

I have known for some time that God wanted me to write a book. Many people that I have prayed with after conducting workshops have approached me saying, "Sister Pendry, you need to write a book." So I began to wait for the right timing from the Lord. God's timing is always perfect (Amen!), so ... here we are. Praise the Lord!

Do you realize there are many people here in America that do not know how to pray? How sad! A nation with so many big churches, but yet the people are so hungry, and a lot of them have not been taught how to seek the face of the Lord with prayer.

> *Then shall ye call upon me, and ye shall go and pray unto me, and I will hearken unto you. And ye shall seek me, and find me, when ye shall search for me with all your heart.* Jeremiah 29:12-13

People are placed in my path all the time that are very good morally, give much to charity, and many are active in church, but have never heard of a repentance prayer.

And they went out, and preached that men should repent. Mark 6:12

You know, God is so good, and I love Him so much because He is so merciful and so full of grace, that He is so delighted to hear us pray to Him to praise Him, to thank Him, and to pray one for another. Hey, this is what life is all about. Hallelujah!

Enter into his gates with thanksgiving, and into his courts with praise: be thankful unto him, and bless His name. For the LORD is good; his mercy is everlasting; and his truth endureth to all generations. Psalm 100:4-5

I hope when you begin to read this book, that you will be blessed, encouraged, inspired, impressed, and that your life will be totally changed by prayer. May the Holy Ghost teach you as you read and pray. Amen!

Thou shalt make thy prayers unto him, and he shall hear thee. Job 22:27

I love you, God bless you! And remember, **don't forget to pray!**

Dr. Pattie Pendry
Raleigh, North Carolina

- 1 -

DID JESUS PRAY?

Yes! Of course Jesus prayed. Not only was He a prayer warrior, but also a prayer teacher. Many times in the Bible Jesus prayed for the disciples. At one point and time He told Peter:

> *Satan hath desired to have you, that he may sift you as wheat: But I have prayed for thee, that thy faith fail not: and when thou art converted, strengthen thy brethren.* Luke 22:31-32

You see, Jesus knew Satan was going to get Peter to tell a lie. You all know that he denied knowing Jesus three times. Now the Lord knew that Simon Peter had a great call on his life, so He was telling him, "Okay, when you become converted (when you have surrendered your life to Me), you will become a dynamic preacher of My Word." Amen!

When Jesus came into this world, He became a role model for us. Therefore if He prayed, we should also.

> *Men ought always to pray and not to faint.*
> Luke 18:1

Did Jesus Pray?

Regardless of the trial or test you are going through, pray. Some people are too lazy to pray. They will say, "I am too tired," or "too sleepy," or "too busy." "Well, honey, I didn't get a chance to pray today, but maybe tomorrow on my lunch hour I will." NO! Every day should be a prayer day!

Do you realize that when you put off praying it is the beginning of backsliding? Excuses will continue to become more plentiful. This is when you are losing the victory, and Satan is gaining it.

> *Evening, and morning, and at noon, will I pray, and cry aloud: and he shall hear my voice.*
> Psalm 55:17

I am glad Jesus never felt that way, aren't you? He went to Gethsemane to pray and took with Him Peter, James, and John (see Mark 14:32-33).

> *And he went forward a little, and fell on the ground and prayed that, if it were possible, the hour might pass from him.*
> Mark 14:35

When Jesus had finished praying, He saw that He prayed alone. The disciples had fallen asleep. Let's not fall asleep but persevere. Amen! Because perseverance availeth much.

Jesus honored His Father with much prayer. It's wonderful how Jesus rejoiced and thanked and praised His Father.

Lord, Teach Me How to Pray

I thank thee, O Father, Lord of heaven and earth, that thou hast hid these things from the wise and prudent, and hast revealed them unto babes: even so, Father; for so it seemed good in thy sight.

Luke 10:21

Oh! Blessed Jesus is so good to us, and He loves us so very much. So let us show Him how much we love Him through prayer, praises, studying His Word, and letting the glory of His light shine through us. Hallelujah!

Do you know the chapter of John 17? Jesus prayed this prayer:

These words spake Jesus, and lifted up his eyes to heaven, and said, Father, the hour is come; glorify thy Son, that thy Son also may glorify thee:
As thou hast given him power over all flesh, that he should give eternal life to as many as thou hast given him.
And this is life eternal, that they might know the only true God, and Jesus Christ, whom thou hast sent.
I have glorified thee on earth: I have finished the work which thou gavest me to do.
And now O Father, glorify me with thine own self with the glory which I had with thee before the world was.

Did Jesus Pray?

I have manifested thy name unto the men which thou gavest me out of the world: thine they were, and thou gavest them me; and they have kept thy word.

Now they have known that all things whatsoever thou hast given me are of thee.

For I have given unto them the words which thou gavest me; and they have received them, and have known surely that I came out from thee, and they have believed that thou didst send me.

I pray for them: I pray not for the world, but for them which thou hast given me, for they are thine.

And all mine are thine, and thine are mine; and I am glorified in them.

And now I am no more in the world, but these are in the world, and I come to thee. Holy Father, keep through thine own name those whom thou hast given me, that they may be one, as we are.

While I was with them in the world, I kept them in thy name: those that thou gavest me I have kept and none of them is lost, but the son of perdition; that the scripture might be fulfilled.

And now come I to thee; and these things I speak in the world that they might have my joy fulfilled in themselves.

I have given them thy word; and the world hath hated them, because they are not of the world, even as I am not of the world.

Lord, Teach Me How to Pray

I pray not that thou shouldest take them out of the world, but that thou shouldest keep them from the evil.

They are not of the world, even as I am not of the world.

Sanctify them through thy truth: thy word is truth.

As thou hast sent me into the world, even so have I also sent them into the world.

And for their sakes I sanctify myself, that they also might be sanctified through the truth.

Neither pray I for these alone, but for them also which shall believe on me through their word;

That they all may be one; as thou, Father, art in me, and I in thee, that they also may be one in us: that the world may believe that thou hast sent me.

And the glory which thou gavest me I have given them; that they may be one even as we are one:

I in them, and thou in me, that they may be made perfect in one; and that the world may know that thou hast sent me, and hast loved them, as thou hast loved me.

Father, I will that they also, whom thou hast given me, be with me where I am; that they may behold my glory, which thou hast given me: for thou lovedst me before the foundation of the world.

O righteous Father, the world hath not known thee: but I have known thee, and these have known that thou hast sent me.

Did Jesus Pray?

And I have declared unto them thy name, and will declare it: that the love wherewith thou hast loved me may be in them, and I in them.

John 17

And they came to a place which was named Gethsemane: and he saith to his disciples, Sit ye here, while I shall pray. Mark 14:32

- 2 -

Jesus Teaches His Disciples How to Pray

And it came to pass in those days that He went out into a mountain to pray, and continued all night in prayer to God.
And when it was day, he called unto him his disciples: and of them he chose twelve whom also he named apostles. You see the disciples wanted to know how to pray.   Luke 6:12-13

And it came to pass that as he was praying in a certain place, when he ceased, one of his disciples said unto him, Lord, teach us how to pray, as John also taught his disciples.   Luke 11:1

Now this is the greatest prayer:

Our Father, which art in heaven, Hallowed be thy name. Thy kingdom come. Thy will be done in earth as it is in heaven. Give us this day our daily bread. And forgive us our debts, as we forgive our debtors. And lead us not into temptation, but deliver

Jesus Teaches His Disciples How to Pray

us from evil: For thine is the kingdom, and the power, and the glory, for ever. Amen.
Matthew 6:9-13

Wow! What a beautiful prayer! How many of you can pray this prayer and really mean it? Huh? Forgiveness, praises, thanking, and wanting Him to deliver you from evil. The devil will set up traps for some of you, and you will walk right into them to fulfill the lust of the flesh. You know what I mean. Now what does this prayer mean?

1. **Our Father:** Once we repent of our sins by being born again (John 3:3), we are then grafted into the family of God. He becomes our Daddy, and we call Him "Our Father."

2. **Hallowed be thy name:** Sanctify, reverence God, lifting Him up to the highest because He is creator of all things.

3. **Thy kingdom come:** Hallelujah! Honey, one day there is going to be a new heaven and a new earth.

And the seventh angel sounded; and there were great voices in heaven, saying, The kingdoms of this world are become the kingdoms of our Lord, and of his Christ; and he shall reign for ever and ever. Revelation 11:15

4. **Thy will be done on earth as it is in heaven:** Oh boy! This is a big one! Now many of you want your prayers to be answered a certain way: "Lord, save my wife, but ... ," "Lord, save my husband, but ... ," or you may say, "Lord, please give me that job at the bank. I want that job so bad!" Ha! Listen to me. Maybe it is not God's will that you have that job. He may have something better for you. Amen!

But, if you don't get that job you prayed for or that house you prayed for, then you begin to question God. "Lord, I had the faith, I prayed about it. Why didn't I get it?" Well, you better start asking God what *His* will is. In other words, allow your will to be broken, so God's will can be manifested and done in your life. And wait patiently for the salvation of those you have prayed for. Remember, God's time clock is different from ours.

5. **Give us this day our daily bread:** All right, how many out there can honestly say you thank God for supplying your food before you ask Him to fill the pantry? My family and I go out quite often to restaurants to eat, and people, I am telling you that you can count on one hand the ones who bless their food before they eat. They just take it for granted. "Well, I just got this job making X number of dollars per week, so I am going to buy and eat what I please." Honey, listen, remember, God is the one that gives you the strength to work. So give Him thanks.

Jesus Teaches His Disciples How to Pray

6. **And forgive us our debts as we forgive our debtors:** Now, when a bill collector calls you on the phone, do you get angry with him and hang up? Listen, that person is only doing his job. You knew before you got in debt and signed that contract that you had to pay that bill. Nobody twisted your arm and made you buy that new car, or furniture, or purchase all those clothes on your charge card. If you don't have the money, then politely tell that bill collector when you can pay it. Then, when you hang up that phone, pray for your debtors.

   How many people have borrowed something from you and never paid you back? Now you know and I know that they haven't forgotten it. Amen! Often times they will see you in a supermarket and they will turn and go another way. Honey, pray for them and forgive them. Because just as sure as the sun shines, they will come to you again for something else. And this time, pray and ask God to give you the wisdom to know what to do.

7. **And lead us not into temptation, but deliver us from evil:** A lot of you put yourselves into situations where you are tempted! Then you blame the Lord. "Oh Father, why did You put this good-looking man in my path?" Or "Why did You put this pretty woman in my path?" Well, you better keep your eyes on Jesus and do like Joseph did. RUN. Amen! (Read Genesis 39:7-18.) Not only did

the devil use Potiphar's wife to tempt him, but she also lied on him. But Joseph remained faithful unto the Lord. This is how we have to be. Don't allow the devil to steal the blessing that God has for you.

How about going into a fast food place, or a department store, and the cashier gives you back too much change. Some of you will say, "Praise the Lord! Look at how He blessed me." Others will just take the money and walk out of the store. That is wrong! Confront that cashier about giving you too much change, because if you don't, her register will come up short, and she will be in trouble. Always do the right thing and God will bless you. Hallelujah!

And be not conformed to this world: but be ye transformed by the renewing of your mind, that ye may prove what is that good, and acceptable, and perfect, will of God. Romans 12:2

Be not overcome of evil, but overcome evil with good. Romans 12:21

8. **For thine is the kingdom, and the power, and the glory forever. Amen!:** It is God's Kingdom, and He has all power, and all glory forever. And, honey, let me tell you, if we continue to praise Him and reverence Him, and to pray, we will reign with Him forever and ever. Amen!

- 3 -

My Experience In Prayer

Let me begin by praising God, and thanking Him for where He has brought me from. God is faithful, and I love Him with all my heart.

I was born in a small town as an only child with an alcoholic daddy and a very domineering mother. Every weekend they would fight. You see, my childhood was not the greatest, but there was one thing I knew for sure: I was not going to be like that when I grew up!

One day I was in the yard playing, and I looked up and saw an airplane. I said, "Lord, please let me ride a plane someday." You see, even then I knew somebody had to be there to send the rain, to have the sun to shine, to make the wild flowers grow. *Amen!*

Oh yes, I would go to church with my mother and grandmother, but they would only want to show off their big, beautiful new hats. I never heard the word repentance. Church was more of a get-together; a "let's talk about people" event.

God knew that when I was a child I had a desire

to serve Him. Years later He placed someone in my life to tell me about Jesus. Honey, I prayed that sinner's prayer, got baptized in the Holy Ghost and, honey I have been running for the Lord ever since! Hallelujah!

God truly answers prayers. I remember when I was going through customs in Israel. A gentleman was going through my Bible when he looked up at me and said, "Lady, if God hears your prayers, please pray for the peace of Israel." I looked at him with tears running down my cheeks and said that God has promised us that one day there will be peace in Israel. *Amen!*

In Russia the Lord had us to pray for many people. Some were deaf, and others could not speak from birth. God worked miracles! The deaf began to hear, and the dumb began to speak. One little boy's first word was alleluia (which means praise).

God sent us to minister in Tennessee, Kentucky, Indiana, Illinois, Missouri, and Kansas. Well, honey, the Spirit of the Lord really moved. This made the devil very mad! Coming back to North Carolina our car gave us trouble. I mean it completely stopped ... in the mountains ... in the dark. Now, honey, you talk about somebody praying? We really prayed! Suddenly we felt a weight lifted from that car and a supernatural strength push from the trunk. That car started up and we drove it home. Praise God! It was the hand of God! You know He tells us:

My Experience In Prayer

And, lo, I am with you alway, even until the end of the world. Matthew 28:20

Once a friend and I went to a mental institution to see someone. Well, of course, when we arrived we prayed and asked Jesus to accompany us. We went in and I introduced myself to the clerk, who in turn called a guard to escort us. Now when she unlocked the elevator, she looked at us very strangely. After visiting with the patient, the same guard escorted us back, giving us another strange look. She asked us, "Where is the other person? When you came in, there were three of you, and now there are only two." That third person she saw was Jesus. People, God still answers prayers!

I had prayed many years for my mother's salvation. How many of you out there know that your family members are the ones you can't minister to? (But you can certainly pray for them.) Amen! Well, Mom got sick and went to the hospital. I would go to see her, take my Bible, and read from it. Well, I did pray a repentance prayer with her, and God spoke to me, "Daughter worry not, for she has made Heaven her home." Don't give up on prayer. Amen!

Therefore I say unto you, What things soever ye desire, when ye pray, believe that ye receive them, and ye shall have them. Mark 11:24

Lord, Teach Me How to Pray

One of my greatest desires is to see souls saved.

One thing I love to do is pray, especially early in the morning, and late at night when everything is very quiet. Also, I have a certain area designated where I pray. Now, don't get me wrong, I pray all through my house, and in my car, and in my yard, and when I am watering my flowers. But I have that certain area that I go to for my quiet time with God.

I have now learned that the more I pray, the more I want to pray. Make your life a tool of prayer, and you will certainly begin to see things change. I remember when I first got saved, I asked Jesus to teach me how to pray, and to teach me His Word. I would say, "Lord, please use me, and let me be more like Jesus each day." You know, that taught me how to die daily to the world and crucify the flesh.

Praying always with all prayer and supplication in the Spirit, and watching thereunto with all perseverance and supplication for all saints.
                                                            Ephesians 6:18

You see, we should never cease from praying. That is the most important thing we can do. Also remember that's the way we communicate with the Father.

When you begin to pray, always reverence God first. Next, thank Him and praise Him for the things He has already done. Then let your request be made

My Experience In Prayer

known unto Him. Always end your prayer in Jesus' name, because He is the mediator between God and man.

> *And the veil of the temple was rent in twain from the top to the bottom. And when the centurion which stood over against him saw that he so cried out, and gave up the ghost, he said, Truly this man was the Son of God.* Mark 15:38-39

You then finish your prayer by saying "Amen," which means "so be it." By saying that, you are claiming the desires of your prayers shall be granted.

> *The desire of the righteous shall be granted.*
> Proverbs 10:24

Do you realize that the more you pray, the closer your walk will be with God? You will walk in the Spirit, and also get great revelation from God!

You see, God does not change; people do. A lot of them don't think Jesus heals today, or works miracles, or supplies our needs today. Oh, honey, yes He does! Just give Him a chance and see Him move by His Spirit.

> *Not by might, nor by power, but by my spirit, saith the LORD of hosts.* Zechariah 4:6

Lord, Teach Me How to Pray

Okay. Let's read in God's Word to see how we can get in His glory, and how we can be changed day by day.

1- See that none render evil for evil unto any man [or anybody]; but ever follow that which is good, both among yourselves and to all men.

2- Rejoice evermore.

3- Pray without ceasing.

4- In every thing give thanks: for this is the will of God in Christ Jesus concerning you.

5- Quench not the Spirit.

6- Despise not prophesyings.

7- Prove all things; hold fast that which is good.

8- Abstain from all appearance of evil.

9- And the very God of peace sanctify you wholly; and I pray God your whole spirit and soul and body be preserved blameless unto the coming of our Lord Jesus Christ.

1 Thessalonians 5:15-23

- 4 -

TEN MEN AND WOMEN WHO PRAYED AND GOT RESULTS

The Bible is filled with stories of men and women who prayed and got results. Let us look at ten of them.

HANNAH PRAYED

Hannah had much to be happy for. Her husband loved her dearly. This fact, however, could not prevent the grief she felt from being unable to bear him a child. When the family want up to the Temple in Shiloh, Hannah, *"prayed unto the Lord and wept sore"* (1 Samuel 1:10). God heard that cry:

Then Eli [the priest] answered and said, Go in peace: and the God of Israel grant thee thy petition that thou hast asked of him. And she said, Let thine handmaid find grace in thy sight. So the woman went her way, and did eat, and her countenance was no more sad.   1 Samuel 1:17-18

Sure, enough, after Hannah and her husband had return home, she became pregnant and bore a son.

His name was called Samuel, and he became the greatest prophet Israel would know in the period of the early judges.

> *Wherefore it came to pass, when the time was come about after Hannah had conceived, that she bare a son, and called his name Samuel, saying, Because I have asked him of the LORD.*
>
> 1 Samuel 1:20

What have you *"asked ... of the Lord"*? He knows the burden of your heart as well and is ready to do the miracle you need today.

MANOAH PRAYED

This type of miracle, although it did not happen every day, was not unique in the life of Hannah. Manoah and his wife had also been childless because she was unable to bear children. One day an angel appeared to his wife and told her to prepare herself because she would conceive and bear a son:

> *There was a certain man of Zorah, of the family of the Danites, whose name was Manoah, and his wife was barren, and bore not. And the angel of the LORD appeared unto the woman, and said unto her, Behold now, thou art barren, and bearest not: but thou shalt conceive, and bear a son.*
>
> Judges 13:2-3

Ten Men and Women Who Prayed and Got Results

God knows the desires of our hearts even before we ask Him for something. The wife of Manoah did conceive and bear a son. He was Samson, the future mighty judge of Israel.

ZACHARIAS PRAYED

The power of God to cause the barren to conceive did not end in Old Testament times. Like Manoah and his wife, Zacharias and Elisabeth who lived in the first century A.D. desired to have children, but could not. Then, one day, Zacharias took the matter to God in prayer:

> *They had no child, because that Elisabeth was barren, and they both were now well stricken in years. And it came to pass, that while he [Zacharias] executed the priest's office before God in the order of his course ... there appeared unto him an angel of the Lord standing on the right side of the altar of incense. ... The angel said unto him, Fear not, Zacharias: for thy prayer is heard; and thy wife Elisabeth shall bear thee a son, and thou shalt call his name John.*   Luke 1:7-8, 11 and 13

Just as the angel had said, Elisabeth, who was both *"barren"* and *"well stricken in years,"* gave birth to a son, and his father named him John. This was the great John the Baptist, who was said, by Jesus, to be greater than any other man born before him. God answers prayer.

ELIJAH PRAYED

Elijah prayed for the dead son of a widow who had befriended him and believed God to restore life to the child:

> *And he cried unto the LORD and said, O LORD my God, hast thou also brought evil upon the widow with whom I sojourn, by slaying her son? And he stretched himself upon the child three times and cried unto the LORD, and said, O LORD my God, I pray thee, let this child's soul come into him again. And the LORD heard the voice of Elijah; and the soul of the child came into him again, and he revived.*   1 Kings 17:20-22

Nothing is impossible with God — if we have faith in Him and are willing to seek Him in prayer. Our God has not changed since the days of Elijah and will answer us, just as He did the prophet.

DANIEL PRAYED

When King Nebuchadnezzar had a dream and was looking for someone to interpret it, he threatened to put to death anyone who gave the wrong

Ten Men and Women Who Prayed and Got Results

answer. This didn't frighten Daniel. He boldly volunteered to get the answer from God.

He went home and told his friends about the king's request so that they could pray with him about this matter, and then he proceeded to enter the throne room of God in prayer. Daniel got results:

Then was the secret revealed unto Daniel in a night vision. Then Daniel blessed the God of heaven.
Daniel 2:19

Daniel was able to visit the king with confidence that he knew the interpretation to the dream. When other people asked him how he was able to interpret the difficult dream when no one else could, he answered them:

There is a God in heaven that revealeth secrets.
Daniel 2:28

That same God is waiting to hear your cry today.

HEZEKIAH PRAYED

King Hezekiah was severely ill. His sickness was said to be *"unto death."* God sent the prophet Isaiah to him to say that his time was very limited and that he would soon die. Isaiah's message to the king was:

Lord, Teach Me How to Pray

Set thine house in order: for thou shalt die, and not live.   Isaiah 38:1

When he heard this message, Hezekiah got serious with God and prayed, and the result was that his life was spared for another fifteen years. God sent Isaiah back with another message for the king:

*Go, and say to Hezekiah, Thus saith the L*ORD*, the God of David thy Father, I have heard thy prayer, I have seen thy tears: behold, I will add unto thy days fifteen years.*   Isaiah 38:5

It happened just as God said it would. Hezekiah not only recovered from his sickness, but he went on to live for fifteen more years. Prayer changes things.

HEZEKIAH PRAYED AGAIN

Some years later, Hezekiah received some threatening letters from the warring Rabshakeh of Assyria, a man who was systematically destroying all the other nations in the region. Hezekiah knew that he would be defenseless against an invading Assyrian force in his own strength, so he took those letters into the house of the Lord and spread them out before God:

Ten Men and Women Who Prayed and Got Results

And Hezekiah prayed unto the LORD.
                                        Isaiah 37:15

When Hezekiah called upon the strength of God, the Almighty responded favorably:

Therefore thus saith the LORD concerning the king of Assyria, He shall not come into this city, nor shoot an arrow there, nor come before it with shields, nor cast a bank against it. By the way that he came, by the same shall he return, and shall not come into this city, saith the LORD. For I will defend this city to save it for mine own sake, and for my servant David's sake.   Isaiah 37:33-35

Hezekiah did not have to send out his forces to face the enemy. Instead, an angel of the Lord went forth and smote the soldiers of the Assyrians:

Then the angel of the LORD went forth, and smote in the camp of the Assyrians a hundred and fourscore and five thousand: and when they arose early in the morning, behold, they were all dead corpses.
                                        Isaiah 37:36

Each of us are faced with enemies who threaten to destroy us, as they have others, but our God is just waiting for our call to send forth His mighty angels to do battle for us. He is still the God of miracles today.

Lord, Teach Me How to Pray

JONAH PRAYED

When the prophet Jonah declined to go where God had instructed him (Ninevah) because he didn't like the people there, God let a great fish swallow him. Fortunately, Jonah got serious with God in prayer in the belly of that great fish:

Then Jonah prayed unto the LORD his God out of the fish's belly. Jonah 2:1

Jonah was understandably in great distress. As he later remembered it, he *"cried"*:

And said, I cried by reason of mine affliction unto the LORD, and he heard me; out of the belly of hell cried I, and thou heardest my voice. For thou hadst cast me into the deep, in the midst of the seas; and the floods compassed me about: all thy billows and thy waves passed over me. Then I said, I am cast out of thy sight; yet I will look again toward thy holy temple. The waters compassed me about, even to the soul: the depth closed me round about, the weeds were wrapped about my head. I went down to the bottoms of the mountains; the earth with her bars was about me for ever: yet hast thou brought up my life from corruption, O LORD my God. When my soul fainted within me I remembered the LORD: and my prayer came in unto thee, into thine holy temple. Jonah 2:2-7

Ten Men and Women Who Prayed and Got Results

Eventually, Jonah was delivered from the belly of the fish:

And the LORD spake unto the fish, and it vomited out Jonah upon the dry land. Jonah 2:10

God sees you in your place of torment, and He has just the right means waiting for your deliverance as well. He is just waiting for you to cry out to Him.

THE FIRST-CENTURY CHRISTIAN BELIEVERS PRAYED

Peter, another of the most important leaders of the fledgling first-century church, was imprisoned and threatened with execution. The members of the church began to pray seriously for his deliverance:

Peter therefore was kept in prison: but prayer was made without ceasing of the church unto God for him. Acts 12:5

This was serious prayer, and God always responds when we mean business with Him. That same night an angel appeared in the prison to set Peter free:

And, behold, the angel of the Lord came upon him, and a light shined in the prison: and he smote Peter on the side, and raised him up, saying, Arise up quickly. And his chains fell off from his hands. And the angel said unto him, Gird thyself, and bind on thy sandals. And so he did. And he saith unto him, Cast thy garment about thee, and follow me. And he went out, and followed him; and wist not that it was true which was done by the angel; but thought he saw a vision. When they were past the first and the second ward, they came unto the iron gate that leadeth unto the city; which opened to them of his own accord: and they went out, and passed on through one street; and forthwith the angel departed from him. Acts 12:7-10

Peter was not only released from prison, but he went on to serve the church for many years afterward. God knows our need and will answer us when we call.

PAUL AND SILAS PRAYED

Paul and Silas were also imprisoned for their faith. They knew what to do:

And at midnight Paul and Silas prayed, and sang praises unto God: and the prisoners heard them.
Acts 16:25

These men were not afraid to die for their faith or to face imprisonment, but they had some serious

Ten Men and Women Who Prayed and Got Results

work to do for the Lord, and they knew that it was not God's will for them to be passing their time in bondage. When they prayed, God immediately answered:

> *And suddenly there was a great earthquake, so that the foundations of the prison were shaken: and immediately all the doors were opened, and every one's bands were loosed.* Acts 16:26

Not only were Paul and Silas set free from the prison, but this miracle caused the jailor and his family to believe as well. If you will learn to pray effectively, God will do miracles for you that will amaze everyone around you and many will be won to the Lord as a result.

The God of those men and women who lived in Bible days is our God as well.

Lord, Teach Me How to Pray. Amen!

SAMPLE PRAYERS WITH GOD'S PROMISED ANSWER

DEAR FATHER,

I THANK YOU FOR ANOTHER DAY. I THANK YOU FOR PEACE THAT YOU GIVE ME IN ALL SITUATIONS. I THANK YOU, LORD, FOR HELPING ME TO REMAIN SILENT TODAY IN MY OFFICE EVEN WHEN I HEARD MY CO-WORKERS TALKING ABOUT ME, BUT I HAVE LEARNED TO LIFT THEM UP TO YOU, TO PRAY FOR THEM. LORD PLEASE TEACH THEM HOW TO WALK IN YOUR HOLY WORD, AND FORGIVE THEM FOR ALL THE UGLY THINGS THEY HAVE SAID AGAINST ME.

IN JESUS' NAME,
AMEN!

Wherefore, my beloved brethren, let every man be swift to hear, slow to speak, slow to wrath: For the wrath of man worketh not the righteousness of God. James 1:19-20

Sample Prayers With God's Promised Answer

LORD,

I JUST PRAISE YOU THIS MORNING, AND I THANK YOU FOR SAVING ME. BLESS THE PEOPLE WHO TAUGHT ME HOW TO BE BORN AGAIN. BUT LORD, MY FAMILY AND FRIENDS DON'T UNDERSTAND ME NOW. THEY SAY I HAVE CHANGED, THAT I AM VERY PECULIAR, JUST BECAUSE I DON'T DO THE THINGS I USED TO DO. PLEASE DROP THE SCALES FROM THEIR EYES SO THAT THEY WILL NOT BE DECEIVED ANY LONGER AND MAY EXPERIENCE THE JOY AND PEACE YOU HAVE GIVEN ME.

IN THE NAME OF JESUS,

AMEN!

But ye are a chosen generation, a royal priesthood, a Holy nation, a peculiar people; that you should shew forth the praises of him who hath called you out of darkness into his marvellous light.
1 Peter 2:9

Lord, Teach Me How to Pray

HOLY FATHER,

I PRAISE YOU AND THANK YOU FOR SUCH A PEACEFUL NIGHT. YOU ARE SO GOOD TO ME, AND I WILL FOREVER PRAISE YOU. I THANK YOU FOR FOOD TO EAT, AND THE FRESH WATER YOU HAVE GIVEN ME TO DRINK. I THANK YOU FOR THE BED I SLEEP IN AND THE CLOTHES THAT I HAVE TO WEAR. I THANK YOU FOR THE DWELLING PLACE THAT I HAVE, AND I THANK YOU FOR MY HEALTH, BECAUSE THERE ARE MANY PEOPLE AROUND THE WORLD THAT ARE LESS FORTUNATE. FATHER, I PRAY FOR THEM. PLEASE SUPPLY ALL THEIR NEEDS, AND BLESS THEM

IN JESUS' NAME,

AMEN!

Giving thanks always for all things unto God and the Father in the name of our Lord Jesus Christ.
                                            Ephesians 5:20

Sample Prayers With God's Promised Answer

PRECIOUS DADDY,

YOU ARE WORTHY TO BE PRAISED, TO RECEIVE GLORY AND HONOR. I THANK YOU, LORD, FOR TELLING ME YOU WILL NEVER LEAVE ME, OR FORSAKE ME, AND THAT YOU WILL MAKE MY CROOKED ROAD STRAIGHT.

TODAY WAS NOT A GOOD DAY FOR ME. THIS MORNING I BURNED THE TOAST, AND I WAS LATE GETTING MY CHILDREN TO SCHOOL BECAUSE I HAD A FLAT TIRE. WHEN I GOT TO WORK, MY BOSS DID NOT UNDERSTAND, BUT I THANK YOU LORD, THAT YOUR GRACE IS SUFFICIENT.

IN JESUS' NAME,

AMEN!

Blessed be God, even the Father of our Lord Jesus Christ, the Father of mercies, and the God of all comfort; Who comforteth us in all our tribulation, that we may be able to comfort them which are in any trouble, by the comfort wherewith we ourselves are comforted of God.
                                    2 Corinthians 1:3-4

Lord, Teach Me How to Pray

LORD,

I JUST LOVE YOU, AND I THANK YOU FOR DELIVERING ME FROM DRUGS. I NEVER REALIZED HOW I WAS DESTROYING MY LIFE, AND HOW I WAS HURTING MY FAMILY, TOO. THE FRIENDS THAT I USE TO HAVE ARE NOT THERE FOR ME ANY LONGER. THEY REFUSE TO COME AROUND. SINCE I HAVE BECOME A CHRISTIAN, EVEN MY PARENTS ARE SAYING THEY WILL NEVER TRUST ME AGAIN.
HOLY FATHER, PLEASE HELP ME. I AM SO LONELY.

IN JESUS' NAME,

AMEN!

When my father and my mother forsake me, then the LORD *will take me up.* Psalm 27:10

Sample Prayers With God's Promised Answer

HEAVENLY FATHER,

I COME BEFORE YOU RIGHT NOW IN THE NAME OF JESUS. I THANK YOU FOR THE STRENGTH YOU GIVE ME DAY BY DAY. I THANK YOU FOR ALWAYS BEING THERE, AND FOR HEARING ME WHEN I PRAY.
FATHER, I AM HURTING VERY BADLY. MY HUSBAND LEFT ME FOR ANOTHER WOMAN. WE WERE MARRIED FOR A LONG TIME, AND I NEVER THOUGHT THIS WOULD EVER HAPPEN. MY HEART IS NOT ONLY HURTING, BUT IT IS BREAKING. LORD, I JUST DON'T KNOW WHAT TO DO ANY MORE. HELP ME.

IN JESUS' NAME,

AMEN!

Beloved, think it not strange concerning the fiery trial which is to try you, as though some strange thing happened unto you: But rejoice, inasmuch as ye are partakers of Christ's sufferings; that, when his glory shall be revealed, ye may be glad also with exceeding joy. **1 Peter 4:12-13**

Lord, Teach Me How to Pray

HOLY FATHER,

I THANK YOU AND I PRAISE YOU. BUT LORD THERE ARE THINGS I JUST DON'T UNDERSTAND. MY CHILDREN ARE VERY REBELLIOUS. THEY DON'T EVEN TREAT ME AS THEIR DADDY. THEY TALK TO ME AS IF I WERE A CHILD, VERY DISRESPECTFUL. LORD, ARE THEY ACTING THIS WAY TOWARD ME BECAUSE I AM A SINGLE PARENT? FATHER, I JUST PLACE THEM INTO YOUR HANDS, KNOWING THAT THERE IS NOTHING TOO HARD FOR YOU TO DO. I REJOICE IN YOU NOW. HALLELUJAH!

IN JESUS' NAME,

AMEN!

The LORD is my rock, and my fortress, and my deliverer; my God, my strength, in whom I will trust; my buckler, and the horn of my salvation and my high tower. Psalm 18:2

Now therefore hearken unto me, O ye children: for blessed are they that keep my ways. Hear instruction, and be wise, and refuse it not.
Proverbs 8:32-33

Sample Prayers With God's Promised Answer

HOLY GOD,

I COME TO YOU THIS MORNING IN THE PRECIOUS NAME OF JESUS. LORD, I LIFT UP YOUR NAME, IN SPITE OF ALL MY FEARS AND TORMENTS.

I PRAISE YOU, LORD, BUT PLEASE DELIVER ME. EVER SINCE I WAS IN THAT AUTOMOBILE ACCIDENT, I AM AFRAID TO DRIVE, I GET PANICKY WHEN I RIDE WITH OTHERS, AND I HAVE EVEN BECOME AFRAID OF THE DARK. AT NIGHT I CANNOT GET TO SLEEP BECAUSE I AM AFRAID OF THE NIGHTMARES I KNOW WILL COME. HELP ME, FATHER.

IN JESUS' NAME,

AMEN!

When thou liest down, thou shalt not be afraid: yea, thou shalt lie down and thy sleep shall be sweet.   Proverbs 3:24

For God hath not given us the spirit of fear; but of power, and of love, and of sound mind.
2 Timothy 1:7

Lord, Teach Me How to Pray

LORD,

I REALLY DON'T KNOW HOW TO PRAY. I'M ONLY TEN YEARS OLD. BUT I JUST WANT MY MOMMY AND DADDY TO STOP DRINKING AND PARTYING AND LEAVING ME HOME ALONE TO TAKE CARE OF MY LITTLE SISTERS. WHEN THEY ARE DRINKING, THEY FIGHT WITH EACH OTHER A LOT. LORD, I JUST WANT MY FAMILY TO LOVE YOU, AND TO TAKE ME PLACES, AND PLAY WITH ME LIKE OTHER PARENTS DO. HELP ME, I PRAY.

IN JESUS' NAME,

AMEN!

But whoso shall offend one of these little ones which believe in me, it were better for him that a millstone were hanged about his neck, and that he were drowned in the depth of the sea.
Matthew 18:6

Sample Prayers With God's Promised Answer

LORD,

I AM A TEENAGER, SIXTEEN YEARS OLD. I AM SO TIRED OF MY PARENTS TELLING ME WHAT TO DO. THEY WANT ME TO GO WITH THEM TO CHURCH EVERY SUNDAY. THEY WON'T LET ME GET MY NOSE PIERCED, OR DO THE THINGS I WANT TO DO. I AM GOING TO RUN AWAY FROM HOME AND LIVE IN THE STREETS. WHAT SHOULD I DO? PLEASE SHOW ME.

IN YOUR NAME,

AMEN!

Sow to yourselves in righteousness, reap in mercy; break up your fallow ground: for it is time to seek the LORD, *till he come and rain righteousness upon you.* Hosea 10:12

Children, obey your parents in all things; for this is well pleasing unto the Lord. Colossians 3:20

Lord, Teach Me How to Pray

DEAR FATHER,

I JUST PRAISE YOUR NAME AND I THANK YOU FOR BEING SO GOOD TO ME. BUT LORD I ASK YOU TO FORGIVE ME, BECAUSE THIS MORNING I HAD AN ATTITUDE WITH MY HUSBAND. HE MADE ME SO UPSET, AND I KNOW I SAID THINGS THAT I SHOULDN'T HAVE. LORD I LOVE MY HUSBAND. PLEASE TEACH ME AND SHOW ME HOW TO BE QUIET.

IN JESUS' NAME,

AMEN!

For thus saith the LORD God, the Holy One of Israel; In returning and rest shall ye be saved; in quietness and confidence shall be your strength: and ye would not. Isaiah 30:15

It is better to dwell in the wilderness, than with a contentious and angry woman.
Proverbs 21:19

Sample Prayers With God's Promised Answer

FATHER,

I JUST WANT TO TELL YOU THAT I LOVE YOU, AND I THANK YOU FOR THIS BEAUTIFUL DAY, AND THE WONDERFUL JOB YOU HAVE GIVEN ME. LORD, PLEASE HELP ME AND DELIVER ME FROM MY ANGER. MY WIFE MADE ME SO MAD THIS MORNING THAT I SLAPPED HER. I DON'T WANT TO ABUSE MY WIFE AND FAMILY. I WOULD LIKE TO BE THE KIND OF HUSBAND AND DADDY THAT MY FAMILY CAN LOOK UP TO. FATHER, PLEASE FORGIVE ME AND HELP ME TO DO BETTER!

IN JESUS' NAME,

AMEN!

And it shall come to pass, that whosoever shall call on the name of the LORD *shall be delivered.*
Joel 2:32

But now ye also put off all these; anger, wrath, malice, blasphemy, filthy communication out of your mouth. Colossians 3:8

Lord, Teach Me How to Pray

BLESSED FATHER,

PRAISE YOUR HOLY NAME. I THANK YOU FOR MY LOVING FAMILY, FOR FOOD AND SHELTER YOU GIVE ME. MY FAMILY HAS GOOD HEALTH AND STRENGTH. BUT LORD I DON'T KNOW WHY I AM JEALOUS OF MY NEIGHBOR'S TRUCK. LORD, WHY CAN'T I AFFORD A NEW TRUCK? I AM WORKING VERY HARD, BUT IT SEEMS THE MORE I WORK, THE LESS I HAVE. WHAT IS WRONG? AM I PRAYING IN VAIN? PLEASE SHOW ME WHAT I AM DOING WRONG.

IN JESUS' NAME,

AMEN!

Rest in the LORD, *and wait patiently for him: fret not thyself because of him who prospereth in his way.* Psalm 37:7

Let this mind be in you, which was also in Christ Jesus. Philippians 2:5

Sample Prayers With God's Promised Answer

OH GOD,

AGAIN I COME TO YOU TO LIFT UP YOUR HOLY NAME. I LOVE YOU WITH ALL MY HEART. I PRAISE YOU AND GLORIFY YOUR NAME. I THANK YOU, JESUS, FOR HEALING MY BODY FROM SICKNESS, AND I WILL ALWAYS PRAISE YOU AND SEEK YOUR FACE CONTINUALLY.

MY MOTHER-IN-LAW SAYS I AM A FANATIC, BUT I JUST PRAY FOR HER TO BE REDEEMED BY THE BLOOD OF THE LAMB. LORD, PLEASE SAVE HER AND TEACH HER TO STOP LYING ABOUT ME.

THANK YOU, LORD.

IN JESUS' NAME,

AMEN!

Blessed are ye, when men shall revile you, and persecute you, and shall say all manner of evil against you falsely, for my sake. Rejoice and be exceeding glad: for great is your reward in heaven: for so persecuted they the prophets which were before you. Matthew 5:11-12

Lord, Teach Me How to Pray

HOLY ONE,

I GIVE YOU THANKS TODAY, LORD. I THANK YOU FOR A SAFE TRIP TO AND FROM THE SUPERMARKET. I THANK YOU FOR PROVIDING THE FINANCES FOR ME TO BUY FOOD. BUT LORD, I FEEL BAD THAT I DIDN'T TELL THAT LADY I MET THAT YOU LOVED HER, AND THAT I WOULD BE PRAYING FOR HER. SHE WAS SO EAGER TO TALK WITH ME ABOUT HER PAIN AND HURT CONCERNING HER SON WHO HAD JUST LOST HIS JOB. LORD, PLEASE FORGIVE ME FOR BEING ASHAMED OF YOU. I DIDN'T WANT TO BE EMBARRASSED. I REPENT OF THAT AND ASK YOU TO HELP ME BE BOLD IN THE FUTURE CONCERNING MY FAITH.

IN JESUS' NAME,

AMEN!

Study to shew thyself approved unto God, a workman that needeth not to be ashamed, rightly dividing the word of truth. **2 Timothy 2:15**

Sample Prayers With God's Promised Answer

HEAVENLY FATHER,

I THANK YOU FOR A BEAUTIFUL DAY, FOR DIRECTING MY PATH, FOR THE FUN MY WIFE AND CHILDREN HAD TODAY ON THE PICNIC. LORD, YOU HAVE GIVEN ME THE MOST WONDERFUL FAMILY A MAN COULD EVER ASK FOR. WE TRUST EACH OTHER, WE LOVE EACH OTHER, AND WE LOVE YOU VERY MUCH BECAUSE YOU HAVE BEEN SO GOOD TO US. I WANT YOU TO TEACH ME HOW TO GET CLOSER TO YOU AND TO BE USED FOR YOUR GLORY.

IN JESUS' NAME,

AMEN!

Let the husband render unto the wife due benevolence: and likewise also the wife unto the husband.
1 Corinthians 7:3

Lord, Teach Me How to Pray

DEAR LORD,

I HAVE NEVER CALLED UPON YOUR NAME BEFORE. MY FAMILY MEMBERS WERE NOT CHRISTIANS, AND I GREW UP IN A HOUSEHOLD WHERE EVERYONE TOOK THE GOOD LIFE FOR GRANTED. MY FAMILY WAS MIDDLE CLASS, WE GOT EVERYTHING WE WANTED, AND I WAS SO CAUGHT UP IN MATERIALISM.

THEN I STARTED HANGING AROUND OTHER YOUNG PEOPLE MY AGE. I THOUGHT THEY WERE COOL — UNTIL THEY STARTED STEALING, AND NOW I'M IN JAIL FOR SOMETHING I DIDN'T EVEN DO.

LORD, PLEASE FORGIVE ME AND HELP ME, I PRAY.

IN JESUS' NAME,

AMEN!

Though I walk in the midst of trouble, thou wilt revive me: thou shalt stretch forth thine hand against the wrath of mine enemies, and thy right hand shall save me. Psalm 138:7

Sample Prayers With God's Promised Answer

OUR FATHER,

I THANK YOU FOR TEACHING ME RIGHT FROM WRONG. I THANK YOU FOR SHOWING ME MY SHORTCOMINGS AND FAILURES. I NEVER REALIZED THAT I WAS PREJUDICED AND THAT I HAD SO MUCH PRIDE. LORD, I'M SORRY. PLEASE FORGIVE ME. I WAS TAUGHT TO ALWAYS LIFT MY HEAD UP HIGH IF PEOPLE AROUND ME WERE OF A DIFFERENT COLOR, OR IF THEY WERE POOR. FATHER, I THANK YOU FOR SHOWING ME THAT YOU HAVE NO RESPECT OF PERSONS, AND THAT ALL PEOPLE ARE CREATED EQUALLY BY YOU.

IN JESUS' NAME,

AMEN!

The fear of the LORD *is to hate evil: pride, and arrogancy, and the evil way, and the froward mouth, do I hate.* Proverbs 8:13

Mine heritage is unto me as a speckled bird. Jeremiah 12:9

Lord, Teach Me How to Pray

MERCIFUL FATHER,

I COME TO YOU WITH PRAISE AND THANKSGIVING. LORD, I NEVER KNEW YOU LOVED ME SO MUCH. I NEVER THOUGHT ANYONE CARED ABOUT ME. THAT IS WHY I TRIED TO COMMIT SUICIDE. BUT GOD, I AM SO GRATEFUL THAT YOU SENT SOMEONE TO ME, AND THEY TOLD ME ABOUT JESUS. THEY ENCOURAGED ME, AND TOLD ME THAT THERE IS HOPE IN ANY SITUATION.

LORD, I THANK YOU FOR THE PEACE AND JOY THAT I HAVE IN MY LIFE NOW. PLEASE CONTINUE TO USE THAT COUPLE TO HELP SOMEONE ELSE LIKE THEY HELPED ME. AND LORD, PLEASE BLESS THEM AND GIVE THEM STRENGTH.

IN JESUS' NAME,

AMEN!

Though ye have lien among the pots, yet shall ye be as the wings of a dove covered with silver, and her feathers with yellow gold. Psalm 68:13

Sample Prayers With God's Promised Answer

BELOVED FATHER,

I GIVE YOU THANKS AND PRAISE THIS MORNING. LORD, YOU KNOW I AM A MEDICAL DOCTOR, MY WIFE IS A NURSE, AND THIS MORNING I AM SCHEDULED FOR TWO OPERATIONS.

LORD, I REALIZE I CAN'T DO ANYTHING WITHOUT YOU, AND EACH TIME I PERFORM SURGERY, THE PATIENT'S LIFE IS IN MY HANDS. FATHER, PLEASE TAKE MY HANDS AND GUIDE THEM AS I USE THE SURGICAL INSTRUMENTS. PLEASE KEEP THESE PATIENTS IN YOUR CARE.

IN JESUS' NAME,

AMEN!

Verily, verily, I say unto you, He that believeth on me, the works that I do shall he do also; and greater works than these shall he do, because I go unto my Father. And whatsoever ye shall ask in my name, that will I do, that the Father may be glorified in the Son. If ye shall ask anything in my name, I will do it. John 14:12-14

Lord, Teach Me How to Pray

DEAR GOD,

I LIFT UP YOUR NAME ABOVE EVERY NAME, BECAUSE YOU ARE WORTHY TO BE PRAISED. LORD, AS YOU KNOW, I AM A LAWYER, AND I HAVE A BUSY DAY TODAY IN THE COURTROOM. I VOW TO CONTINUE TO BE HONEST, REGARDLESS OF THE COST.

I PRAY FOR MY CLIENTS, BECAUSE THEY ARE ALL GOING THROUGH DIFFICULT TIMES. LORD, PLEASE BE WITH ME TODAY. GIVE ME STRENGTH, AND TEACH ME WHAT TO SAY AND HOW TO SAY IT.

IN THE NAME OF JESUS,

AMEN!

Let your speech be alway with grace, seasoned with salt, that ye may know how ye ought to answer every man. Colossians 4:6

Sample Prayers With God's Promised Answer

LORD,

THANK YOU FOR ALWAYS BEING THERE FOR ME. LORD, YOU KNOW THAT BEING A SCHOOL TEACHER IS NOT EASY AND, WITH MY HUSBAND BEING A PRINCIPAL, WE HAVE SUCH A GREAT DECISION TO MAKE.

WE MAY NOT BE ALLOWED TO PRAY IN THE PUBLIC SCHOOLS, BUT, PRAISE GOD, WE CAN PRAY FOR THE STAFF AND STUDENTS AT HOME. FATHER, I LIFT THEM ALL UP TO YOU NOW. PLEASE LET THEM KNOW WE CARE ABOUT THEM. TEACH US HOW TO REACH OUT TO THEM. LET THEM SEE THAT WE ARE DIFFERENT. WE WANT OUR LIGHT TO SHINE AMONG THEM FOR YOUR GLORY.

IN JESUS' NAME,

AMEN!

Let your light so shine before men, that they may see your good works, and glorify your Father which is in heaven.   Matthew 5:16

The hand of our God is upon all them for good that seek him; but his power and his wrath is against all them that forsake him.   Ezra 8:22

Lord, Teach Me How to Pray

OH, LORD,

THANK YOU FOR BEING WITH ME YESTERDAY WHILE I WAS ON THE ROAD. I AM NOT A CHRISTIAN, AND I DON'T KNOW HOW TO PRAY.

MY OLD MAN TAUGHT ME HOW TO BE STRONG, BOLD, AND TOUGH, BUT I'M SCARED. YOU SEE, I'M A TRUCK DRIVER, AND TWO OF MY BUDDIES GOT KILLED A COUPLE OF WEEKS AGO WHILE DRIVING THEIR RIGS.

I DON'T WANT NOTHING TO HAPPEN TO ME. I DON'T WANT TO LEAVE THIS WORLD ALONE AND AFRAID. YOU SEE, I'M NOT REALLY STRONG, I'M WEAK. EVEN THOUGH I'M A BIG MAN, I STILL CRY. WELL, NOW I'M CRYING FOR HELP. PLEASE SAVE ME.

IN JESUS' NAME,

AMEN!

He will be very gracious unto thee at the voice of thy cry; when he shall hear it, he will answer thee.
Isaiah 30:19

The name of the LORD is a strong tower: the righteous runneth into it, and is safe.
Proverbs 18:10

Sample Prayers With God's Promised Answer

HEAVENLY FATHER,

I GIVE THANKS TONIGHT, AND I BLESS YOUR NAME FOR GIVING ME SUCH A BEAUTIFUL DAY. LORD, HELP ME NOT TO WORRY AND COMPLAIN. IT SEEMS THAT I WORRY ALL THE TIME ABOUT MY CHILDREN, ABOUT MY HOUSE PAYMENT, AND ABOUT LOSING MY JOB. MY HUSBAND SAYS ALL I DO IS NAG AND COMPLAIN. LORD, HELP ME AND TEACH ME HOW TO BE CONTENT.

IN JESUS' NAME,

AMEN!

Let your conversation be without covetousness; and be content with such things as ye have: for he hath said, I will never leave thee, nor forsake thee.
Hebrews 13:5

Therefore I say unto you, Take no thought for your life, what ye shall eat, or what ye shall drink; nor yet for your body, what ye shall put on. Is not the life more than meat, and the body than raiment? ... Take therefore no thought for the morrow: for the morrow shall take thought for the things of itself. Sufficient unto the day is the evil thereof.
Matthew 6:25 and 34

Lord, Teach Me How to Pray

DEAR GOD,

LET ME BEGIN BY PRAISING YOU AND THANKING YOU FOR BEING WHO YOU ARE, AND FOR WHAT YOU MEAN TO ME. FATHER, I HAVE A VERY LONG FLIGHT TODAY AND, BEING AN AIRPLANE PILOT WITH A PLANE FULL OF PASSENGERS MAKES ME RESPONSIBLE FOR A LOT OF LIVES. ACCORDING TO THE WEATHER REPORT, THERE WILL BE BAD THUNDERSTORMS AND HIGH WINDS. LORD, PLEASE PROTECT ME AND MY PASSENGERS TODAY. TAKE MY HANDS AND HOLD THEM TIGHT AS I FLY THAT PLANE. OH, FATHER, BETTER STILL, YOU BE THE PILOT, AND I WILL BE THE COPILOT. BLESS THE FLIGHT ATTENDANTS ALSO.

IN JESUS' NAME,

AMEN!

In righteousness shalt thou be established: thou shalt be far from oppression; for thou shalt not fear: and from terror; for it shall not come near thee.
Isaiah 54:14

And he saith unto them, Why are ye fearful, O ye of little faith? Then he arose, and rebuked the winds and the sea; and there was a great calm.
Matthew 8:26

Sample Prayers With God's Promised Answer

LORD,

THANK YOU FOR ANSWERING PRAYERS AND FOR BEING THERE FOR ME. PRAISE YOUR HOLY NAME. TODAY IS A HOLIDAY FOR SOME WORKERS, BUT NOT FOR ME. I STILL HAVE TO DELIVER THE MAIL, WHICH IS VERY HEAVY. IT IS ALSO VERY HOT AND HUMID, AND MANY OF THE HOMES HAVE DOGS THAT TRY TO BITE ME. PLEASE LORD, GIVE ME STRENGTH AND PROTECTION, AND BE WITH ME AS I WALK AND DELIVER THIS MAIL.
I LOVE YOU.

IN JESUS' NAME,

AMEN!

For I the LORD thy God will hold thy right hand, saying unto thee, Fear not. I will help thee.
Isaiah 41:13

The LORD is my strength and my shield; my heart trusted in him, and I am helped: therefore my heart greatly rejoiceth; and with my song will I praise him. Psalm 28:7

Lord, Teach Me How to Pray

LORD,

WE THANK YOU FOR PROTECTING US. WE HAVE BEEN OUT ON THE STREETS AT ALL TIMES OF THE NIGHT DOING THINGS THAT WE KNOW ARE VERY WRONG. WE ARE ALL JUST TEENAGERS TRYING TO BE COOL, BAD, AND REBELLIOUS.

WE HAVE GOTTEN IN TROUBLE AND NEVER GOTTEN CAUGHT. LORD, PLEASE HELP US TO FIND A WAY OUT. I AM VERY SORRY AS CAN BE FOR ALL OF THE HEARTACHE I HAVE CAUSED YOU. PLEASE SAVE MY GIRLFRIEND, AND TEACH HER, TOO, SO SHE CAN HAVE MERCY AND GRACE WITH YOU.

TEACH US HOW TO PRAY A SINNER'S PRAYER SO THAT OUR LIVES WILL NO LONGER BE IN DESPAIR. WE ARE TIRED OF HURTING AND BEING BAD. PLEASE GIVE US THE PEACE THAT WE HAVE NEVER HAD. FORGIVE US OF OUR SINS.

IN JESUS' NAME,

AMEN!

Now the Lord of peace Himself give you peace always by all means. The Lord be with you all.
2 Thessalonians 3:16

Sample Prayers With God's Promised Answer

DEAR FATHER,

I TRUST YOU, AND I THANK YOU FOR SPARING MY LIFE. I AM GOING TO BE HONEST WITH YOU NOW. ALL MY LIFE I HAVE BEEN SEXUALLY ABUSED. TODAY I AM TWENTY-FIVE YEARS OLD, AND I AM STILL BEING ABUSED BY MY SPOUSE.
I AM FULL OF HATE, ANGER, BITTERNESS, UNFORGIVENESS, AND THERE HAVE BEEN TIMES WHEN I WANTED TO END EVERYONE'S LIVES AROUND ME, INCLUDING MY OWN. PLEASE TEACH ME HOW TO LOVE, TRUST, AND FORGIVE. I AM BEING TOTALLY DESTROYED. THANK YOU, LORD.

IN JESUS' NAME,

AMEN!

My flesh and my heart faileth: but God is the strength of my heart, and my portion for ever.
Psalm 73:26

And it shall come to pass in the day that the LORD shall give thee rest from thy sorrow, and from thy fear, and from the hard bondage wherein thou wast made to serve. Isaiah 14:3

Lord, Teach Me How to Pray

Let all bitterness, and wrath, and anger, and clamour, and evil speaking, be put away from you, with all malice: And be ye kind one to another, tenderhearted, forgiving one another, even as God for Christ's sake hath forgiven you.

Ephesians 4:31-32

Sample Prayers With God's Promised Answer

BLESSED FATHER,

I TRULY THANK YOU FOR MY WEDDING WHICH TAKES PLACE TODAY. I CONSIDER MYSELF BLESSED, MARRYING MY CHILDHOOD SWEETHEART, AND HAVING BOTH OUR PARENTS AS FRIENDS AND NEIGHBORS. LORD, BLESS OUR MARRIAGE. CONTINUE TO TEACH US HOW TO RESPECT EACH OTHER, TO TRUST EACH OTHER, TO BE HONEST WITH EACH OTHER, TO LISTEN TO EACH OTHER. LORD, WE WANT TO BE IN ONE ACCORD IN EVERYTHING WE DO. LET US GROW IN LOVE EACH DAY, BUT, MOST OF ALL, IN OUR LOVE FOR YOU.
FATHER, BE THE HEAD OF OUR HOUSEHOLD. THANK YOU FOR THAT.

IN JESUS' NAME,

AMEN!

And the LORD God said, It is not good that the man should be alone; I will make him an help meet for him. Genesis 2:18

For this cause shall a man leave his father and mother, and shall be joined unto his wife, and they two shall be one flesh. Ephesians 5:31

Lord, Teach Me How to Pray

DEAR GOD,

THANKS AND PRAISES BE UNTO YOU FOREVER. YOU ARE SO GOOD TO ME, BLESS YOUR HOLY NAME.

AS YOU KNOW, LAST NIGHT WAS A ROUGH NIGHT FOR ME. BEING A POLICEMAN ISN'T EASY, BUT SOMEONE HAS TO DO IT. FATHER, I THANK YOU FOR MY PROTECTION WHILE I AM OUT THERE. I ALSO THANK YOU FOR BEING THERE AND TAKING CARE OF MY FAMILY WHILE I AM AT WORK.

LORD, I PRAY FOR ALL THE INMATES. SOME ARE HURTING VERY BADLY. THEY THINK THERE IS NOBODY WHO CARES FOR THEM. MANY ARE SUFFERING FROM REJECTION. LORD, PLEASE LET THEM KNOW THAT YOU LOVE THEM AND YOU WANT TO HELP THEM, AND IF THEY WOULD ONLY GIVE THEIR LIFE TO YOU THEY WILL HAVE INNER PEACE WHICH NO MAN TAKETH AWAY.

IN JESUS' NAME,
AMEN!

But God commendeth his love toward us, in that, while we were yet sinners, Christ died for us.
Romans 5:8

Sample Prayers With God's Promised Answer

I am not come to call the righteous, but sinners to repentance.   Matthew 9:13

I exhort therefore, that first of all, supplications, prayers, intercessions, and giving of thanks be made for all men; For kings, and for all that are in authority; that we may lead a quiet and peaceable life in all Godliness and honesty. For this is good and acceptable in the sight of God our Saviour; Who will have all men to be saved, and to come unto the knowledge of the truth. For there is one God, and one mediator between God and men, the man Christ Jesus.   1 Timothy 2:1-5

We all have much to learn about prayer.
Lord, Teach Me How to Pray. Amen!

- 6 -

My Prayer for Anorexics and Bulimics

If we could overhear the prayer of an anorexic person, it might sound something like this:

DEAR FATHER,

I THANK YOU FOR GIVING ME A CHRISTIAN MOTHER AND A BROTHER AND SISTER WHO LOVE ME. THANK YOU FOR GIVING ME A RESTFUL NIGHT LAST EVENING.

LORD, I REALLY NEED YOUR HELP. YOU SEE, I AM ANOREXIC. I WANT TO EAT, BUT JUST CAN'T. ALSO, MY BEST FRIEND IS BULIMIC. SHE EATS, BUT THEN SHE SPITS IT ALL BACK UP.

OH FATHER, HOW DID THIS STRONGHOLD COME UPON ME? IF I CAN'T EAT I WILL DIE. MY FRIEND HAS TERRIBLE NIGHTMARES. WE BOTH HAVE LOTS OF FEARS, AND I REALLY DON'T KNOW WHAT TO DO.

My Prayer for Anorexics and Bulimics

AS I LOOK BACK, I CAN REMEMBER THAT WHEN I WAS FIVE YEARS OLD OTHER KIDS WOULD TEASE ME AND CALL ME FAT. I WOULD CRY AND RUN TO MY MOTHER. SHE WOULD ALWAYS COMFORT AND PROTECT ME, BUT LORD, NOW I AM GROWN. I ONLY WEIGH NINETY-FOUR POUNDS NOW AND AM VERY WEAK. PLEASE HEAL AND DELIVER MY FRIEND AND ME, BECAUSE WE REALLY NEED YOUR HELP. LORD I AM TRUSTING IN YOU BECAUSE I KNOW YOU CAN DO ANYTHING, AND YOU ARE ALL POWERFUL. THANK YOU, FATHER, FOR LISTENING TO MY PRAYER.

IN JESUS' NAME,

AMEN!

I have good news for the all those suffering from anorexia or bulimia. God has promised:

Fear not, little flock; for it is your Father's good pleasure to give you the kingdom. Luke 12:32

Every moving thing that liveth shall be meat for you; even as the green herb have I given you all things. Genesis 9:3

Lord, Teach Me How to Pray

If ye be willing and obedient, ye shall eat the good of the land.   Isaiah 1:19

If I were hungry, I would not tell thee: for the world is mine, and the fulness thereof.

Psalm 50:12

When Jesus encountered people who were hungry, He fed them:

But Jesus said unto them, They need not depart; give ye them to eat. And they say unto him, We have here but five loaves, and two fishes. He said, Bring them hither to me. And he commanded the multitude to sit down on the grass and took the five loaves, and the two fishes, and looking up to heaven, he blessed, and brake, and gave the loaves to his disciples, and the disciples to the multitude. And they did all eat, and were filled.

Matthew 14:16-20

He died on the cross to set us free from every bondage, including anorexia and bulimia:

And that they may recover themselves out of the snare of the devil, who are taken captive by him at his will.   2 Timothy 2:26

Anorexia and bulimia is a deception. God has provided food for us to eat. In the very beginning,

My Prayer for Anorexics and Bulimics

He developed a beautiful garden and placed man there to partake freely of its fruit:

> *And out of the ground made the LORD God to grow every tree that is pleasant to the sight, and good for food.* Genesis 2:9

God doesn't want anyone to starve themselves to death. That would please the devil, but it grieves the heart of God. Satan is a deceiver, and he wants to destroy everyone he can. Jesus said of him:

> *The thief cometh not, but for to steal, and to kill, and to destroy: I am come that they might have life, and that they might have it more abundantly.* John 10:10

We don't find a single case in biblical history of a person who loved God dying for lack of food. Please allow Jesus to help you and deliver you from this bondage. Jesus loves you, and He is always there for you.

When Elijah was hungry, God sent ravens to feed him:

> *And the ravens brought him bread and flesh in the morning, and bread and flesh in the evening; and he drank of the brook.* 1 Kings 17:6

When Moses and the children of Israel were hun-

Lord, Teach Me How to Pray

gry in the wilderness, God sent them manna from Heaven. When that was not satisfying to them, God sent them quail in abundance:

> *And the Lord spake unto Moses, saying, I have heard the murmurings of the children of Israel: speak unto them, saying, At even ye shall eat flesh, and in the morning ye shall be filled with bread and ye shall know that I am the LORD your God. And it came to pass, that at even the quails came up, and covered the camp: and in the morning the dew lay round about the host. And when the dew that lay was gone up, behold, upon the face of the wilderness there lay a small round thing, as small as hoar frost on the ground. And when the children of Israel saw it, they said one to another, It is manna: for they wist not what it was. And Moses said unto them, This is the bread which the LORD hath given you to eat.* Exodus 16:11-15

If God did not want us to eat, why would He provide food for us?

I want to pray for you now, remembering the promise of our Lord:

> *Again I say unto you, That if two of you shall agree on earth as touching any thing that they shall ask, it shall be done for them of my Father which is in heaven.* Matthew 18:19

My Prayer for Anorexics and Bulimics

OH, HOLY GOD OF ABRAHAM, ISAAC, AND JACOB,

INCLINE YOUR EAR TO US THIS DAY, WE PRAY, FOR WE EARNESTLY SEEK YOUR FACE. WE LIFT UP BEFORE YOU ALL THOSE WHO ARE SUFFERING FROM ANOREXIA AND BULIMIA, AND WE COMMAND EVERY BONDAGE OF DARKNESS TO BE BROKEN IN THEIR LIVES.

FATHER, YOU HAVE COMMANDED US TO PRAY FOR ONE ANOTHER, AND SO WE LIFT UP OUR BROTHERS AND SISTERS WHO NEED OUR HELP IN PRAYER, AND WE DO IT IN THE MIGHTY NAME OF JESUS.

THESE PEOPLE HAVE BEEN DECEIVED, OPPRESSED, AND DEPRESSED BY SATAN'S POWER TOO LONG. FATHER, SET THEM FREE THAT THEY MAY HAVE THE LIBERTY THAT HAS BEEN PROMISED TO THEM BY YOUR HOLY WORD. WE DECLARE IT TO BE SO, WE DECREE A MIRACLE FOR EACH ONE OF THEM, AND WE CLAIM IT DONE.

IN JESUS' MIGHTY NAME,

AMEN!

- 7 -

MY PRAYER FOR PASTORS

Woe be unto the pastors that destroy and scatter the sheep of my pasture! saith the LORD. Therefore thus saith the LORD God of Israel against the pastors that feed my people; Ye have scattered my flock, and driven them away, and have not visited them: behold, I will visit upon you the evil of your doings, saith the LORD. And I will gather the remnant of my flock out of all countries wither I have driven them, and will bring them again to their folds; and they shall be fruitful and increase. And I will set up shepherds over them which shall feed them: and they shall fear no more, nor be dismayed, neither shall they be lacking, saith the LORD.

Jeremiah 23:1-4

God has pronounced woe upon many pastors, those whose eyes are not on guarding the flock, but on gaining material possessions; those who are walking, talking, dressing, and acting like the world; those who are lying and deceiving God's little ones. Who do they think they are trying to fool? God knows their hearts and cannot be fooled.

My Prayer for Pastors

If you are one of those pastors who are more concerned about the number of people who join your church than about the salvation of their souls, if you are one of those who are intent upon constructing a three-million-dollar building with gold-plated light fixtures and crystal chandeliers, if you are one of those who gauge the preaching by how it will be received by a few of the wealthiest members, if you are one of those who believe they have to drive a fifty-thousand-dollar car because their members are well educated and live in the nicer part of town, if you are one of those who are ashamed to have people from the wrong side of the tracks attend your services, then I have news for you. God has pronounced woe on your life and ministry.

You need to repent and humble yourself before the Lord, or your pride is going to destroy you and take you down. Ask God right now to fill your heart with His love, a love that has no respect of persons. Ask Him to drop the scales from your eyes so you will begin to see with spiritual eyes. Ask Him to teach you how to walk in the Spirit and not in the flesh.

A young lady I know was prevented from entering a certain church by the ushers because she was of the wrong color. A young man who was trying to get free of drugs went to church, trusting that the people there could help him. Because he had long hair that he kept in a pony tail and an earring in one ear, he was not received there. May the Lord have mercy on us all.

The Bible says in the book of Revelation:

> *And the Spirit and the bride say, Come. And let him that heareth say, Come. And let him that is athirst come. And whosoever will, let him take the water of life freely.* Revelation 22:17

God didn't say we had to be rich or well educated or well dressed or of a certain color in order to come to Him, His invitation is *"Come ... whosoever will"* and that must be our invitation as well. Once people get cleaned up on the inside, then God will teach them how to get cleaned up on the outside. Praise the Lord!

If you build a big and beautiful house but put nothing in it, those who passed by the outside might be impressed and might say, "Wow! That is the most beautiful house I have ever seen!" But, if one of them were to come inside and find the house empty, with not even a single chair to sit in, they would no longer be impressed. What good is a house like that?

Jesus taught:

> *When the unclean spirit is gone out of a man, he walketh through dry places, seeking rest, and*

My Prayer for Pastors

findeth none. Then he saith, I will return into my house from whence I came out; and when he is come, he findeth it empty, swept, and garnished. Then goeth he and taketh with himself seven other spirits more wicked than himself, and they enter in and dwell there: and the last state of that man is worse than the first. Matthew 12:43-45

Pastors, it is time to stop preaching the things people want to hear and start preaching the truth, as God gives it. God will hold you responsible for all those souls He has placed under your care. It is an awesome responsibility, and it is time you took it seriously.

Pastors, let me pray for you!

OH, HOLY GOD,

I COME TO YOU NOW IN THE NAME OF JESUS. I THANK YOU FOR SAVING US, LORD AND FOR GIVING US ETERNAL LIFE AND THE PRIVILEGE OF SERVING YOU. NOW, LORD, HELP EVERY PASTOR TO REALIZE THE AWESOME RESPONSIBILITY YOU HAVE PLACED UPON THEM. OPEN THEIR SPIRITUAL EYES THAT THEY MIGHT UNDERSTAND WHAT IS TRULY IMPORTANT. MAY PASTORS EVERY-

Lord, Teach Me How to Pray

WHERE SEEK YOU WITH ALL THEIR HEARTS. MAY THE FEAR OF GOD FALL UPON THEM. MAY THEY DIE TO THE WORLD, SO THE SPIRIT OF GOD CAN RISE UP IN THEM, SO THAT THEY CAN BE MIGHTY WARRIORS FOR YOU. MAY THEY PREACH THE GOSPEL FAITHFULLY AND WIN SOULS FOR YOUR KINGDOM.

IN JESUS' NAME,

AMEN!

Lord, Teach Me How to Pray. **Amen!**

- 8 -

MY PRAYER FOR POLITICIANS

That at the name of Jesus every knee should bow, of things in heaven, and things in earth, and things under the earth; and that every tongue should confess that Jesus Christ is Lord, to the glory of God the Father. Philippians 2:10-11

The Bible has much to say to persons of high authority, and the most important thing is that each and every one must realize his or her need of God. Without God, we can do nothing and, therefore, we must seek Him in prayer before making any decision. Without God and His strength, we would be helpless to even tie our shoes laces.

The idea of the separation of church and state that many are espousing is simply erroneous. You cannot leave God out of anything and expect it to do well. If it were not for God, there would be no state. If it were not for God, there would be no Earth. God's Word shows us:

In the beginning God created the heaven and the earth. Genesis 1:1

Lord, Teach Me How to Pray

We simply must honor God and never be ashamed of Him. Those who put Him first in everything will be blessed.

Many decades ago it was decided by officials of this country to put the words, "In God we trust" on all our coins, showing that, as a nation, we recognized that without Him we were nothing. What happened to that trust in God? Now we seem to trust in everything else but Him.

Prayer has been taken out of our schools and sex has been put in. Students cannot bless their food in the cafeteria because such a prayer might be offensive to other students, and they are forbidden to wear a t-shirt that has a quotation from the Bible or something about Jesus on it, but they can wear a shirt with something demonic written on it. We had better wake up before it's too late.

Life is short and each of us must answer to God:

And as it is appointed unto men once to die, but after this the judgment. Hebrews 9:27

One day, *"every knee [will] bow"* and *"every tongue [will] confess that Jesus Christ is Lord."* What will your status be on that day?

Paul declared to the sophisticated Romans:

For it is written, As I live, saith the Lord, every knee shall bow to me, and every tongue shall con-

My Prayer for Politicians

fess to God. So then every one of us shall give account of himself to God. Romans 14:11-12

What a terrible thought for some!

I have had the privilege of giving the invocation at many political gatherings and have met and prayed with many politicians. Gratefully, I have been blessed to see many of them reaching out to God for help. But wouldn't it be great to see all of them reaching out to God in prayer?

When we have more people agreeing together, there is strength. The Scriptures teach that if one can chase away a thousand enemies, two can *"put ten thousand to flight"*:

> *How should one chase a thousand, and two put ten thousand to flight, except their Rock had sold them, and the LORD had shut them up.*
> Deuteronomy 32:30

God honors and lifts us those who trust Him. He said:

> *For I will have respect unto you, and make you fruitful, and multiply you, and establish my covenant with you.* Leviticus 26:9

If we will just get off the devil's bandwagon and

Lord, Teach Me How to Pray

get on the chariot with Jesus, we will begin to see great and mighty things happen. He declared:

> *If my people, which are called by my name, shall humble themselves, and pray, and seek my face, and turn from their wicked ways; then will I hear from heaven, and will forgive their sin, and will heal their land.*   2 Chronicles 7:14

God is still on the throne, and you must let Him be God. Here is God's message for politicians:

> *Thus saith the* LORD, *Let not the wise man glory in his wisdom, neither let the mighty man glory in his might, let not the rich man glory in his riches: But let him that glorieth glory in this, that he understandeth and knoweth me, that I am the* LORD *which exercise lovingkindness, judgment, and righteousness in the earth: for in these things I delight, saith the* LORD.   Jeremiah 9:23-24

Politicians, let me pray for you:

HOLY FATHER,

I COME TO YOU IN THE PRECIOUS NAME OF JESUS. I LIFT UP EVERY POLITICAL LEADER TO YOU. PLEASE SPEAK TO THEIR HEARTS. TEACH THEM TO LOOK

My Prayer for Politicians

TO YOU. LET THEM KNOW THAT THEY ALL WILL BE SHAKING BY YOUR SPIRIT. MAY THEY KNOW THE TRUTH AND LIVE IT.

IN JESUS' NAME,

AMEN!

Lord, Teach Me How to Pray. Amen!

- 9 -

A Prayer of Repentance

The Lord is not slack concerning his promise, as some men count slackness; but is longsuffering to us-ward, not willing that any should perish, but that all should come to repentance.

2 Peter 3:9

Nothing could be more important than a prayer of repentance. God doesn't demand perfection of us, but He does demand that we recognize our failures and our need of Him.

When the disciples first went out preaching, the message they carried everywhere was one of repentance:

And they went out, and preached that men should repent. Mark 6:12

Each of us, at some point in our lives, must pray the sinner's prayer and accept Jesus as our personal Lord and Savior.

If you have never been born again, please pray with me this prayer of repentance:

A Prayer of Repentance

LORD JESUS,

COME INTO MY HEART.
FORGIVE ME OF ALL MY SINS.
THOUGH MY SINS BE "AS SCARLET," MAKE THEM "WHITE AS SNOW."
THOUGH THEY BE "LIKE CRIMSON," MAKE THEM "WHITE LIKE WOOL."
JESUS, PLEASE DELIVER ME FROM ALL MY BAD HABITS.
DELIVER ME FROM ALL MY FEARS AND TORMENTS.
TAKE ME BY THE HAND, LEAD ME, GUIDE ME, AND WALK WITH ME EACH DAY.
THANK YOU, LORD, FOR WRITING MY NAME IN THE LAMB'S BOOK OF LIFE.
I LOVE YOU, JESUS, AND I WILL LIVE FOR YOU FROM THIS DAY FORTH.

IN YOUR NAME I PRAY,

AMEN!

If you sincerely prayed that prayer, you are now a child of God and can walk daily with the Lord at your side. The new life you feel in you is from Him, so don't try to live this Christian life without His help. You simply can't do it.

This is such a short book, and there is much more

to learn about prayer. If you are willing to talk to God and to read His Word, He will teach you day by day.

> *The Lord is not slack concerning his promise, as some men count slackness; but is longsuffering to us-ward, not willing that any should perish, but that all should come to repentance.*
> **2 Peter 3:9**

Never hesitate to say to Him, *Lord, Teach Me How to Pray.*

One of his disciples said unto him, LORD, TEACH US TO PRAY, as John also taught his disciples. **Luke 11:1**

POEMS

BY
DR. PATTIE PENDRY

Poems by Dr. Pattie Pendry

STRENGTH

What would I do if it wasn't for Jesus
Who gives me strength each day?
What would I do if He wasn't there
To lead and show me the way?

He is always there to lift me up
When I feel loaded down.
And He takes my hand and guides my feet
And leads me to higher ground.

He says, "My child, don't worry,
"For I am always there for you.
"Yes, tomorrow is another day,
"But I have promised to see you through."

Sure, My strength is sufficient
And My love for you is wide.
Abide in Me, and in My Word.
You will always be near My side.

I will lift you up as an eagle,
And I will place you on the highest peak.
You will receive the strength you have never had
To make My voice complete.

You will open your mouth and praise Me
As you tell others what I have done for thee.
For My love and strength is forever.
That is why I died upon the tree.

Copyright © 1997 — Dr. Pattie Pendry

Lord, Teach Me How to Pray

PRAISE ME, SAITH THE LORD

Praise Me, saith the Lord,
In the darkness of the night.
Praise Me, saith the Lord,
And know that everything's all right.
Praise Me, saith the Lord,
As I hold your hand real tight.
Praise Me, saith the Lord,
As My light shines through the night.
Praise Me, saith the Lord,
And the sun will shine on a cloudy day.
Praise Me, saith the Lord,
And all the dark clouds shall roll away.
Praise Me, saith the Lord,
As the tears are wiped away from your eyes.
Praise Me, saith the Lord,
So we can both be in one accord.
Praise Me, saith the Lord,
And I will supply all your needs.
Praise Me, saith the Lord,
As I record all your good deeds.
Praise Me, saith the Lord,
As you see the rainbow in the sky.
Praise Me, saith the Lord,
As you watch Me as I go by.
Praise Me, saith the Lord,
As the birds that cry out to Me.
Praise Me, saith the Lord,
So you can walk in victory.
Praise Me, saith the Lord.

Copyright ©1997 — Dr. Pattie Pendry

Poems by Dr. Pattie Pendry

GIVE THANKS

Are you ever too tired to open your mouth
Or whisper a silent prayer,
To lift up your hands and praise His name
And thank Him for being there?

Are you ever too tired to reach out to Him
And thank Him for your food,
Or give Him thanks for the bed you have
That He has placed in your room?

Are you too tired to look up to Him
And thank Him for your clothes
That He has placed inside your room
To keep you nice and warm?

Have you given Him thanks for the health that you have?
Are you taking it for granted too,
Not recognizing all the works He has done
And all He has done for you?

Are you too busy to give Him thanks
For giving you another day
Or going ahead with your daily tasks
Forgetting Him all the way?

Please lift up your voice and give Him thanks

Lord, Teach Me How to Pray

For all that He has done.
Remember, He is the One who has given you feet
To stand, to walk, and to run.
Give God thanks from day to day
and praise His holy name.
Give Him thanks for saving your soul
And touching you and making you whole.

Give Thanks!

Copyright © — 1996 Dr. Pattie Pendry

Poems by Dr. Pattie Pendry

GOD'S IN CONTROL

Have you ever watched the flowers
How they began to grow
Or seen the trees so tall and green
How they rock to and fro?

Have you seen the grass so green and wet
That God has sent from His Heaven's best
Or watched the birds as they fly and sing
And thanked the Lord that Jesus reigns?

Have you watched the sun how it rises and sets
By God's own time clock too
That He made to beautify in this world?
He made for me and you.

Have you seen the stars that shine at night
Or see the moon so full and bright
And heard the crickets as they talk and sing?
They are all lifting up Jesus' name.

Have you ever seen the ocean so big and wide?
We never can see on the other side.
And watched the seagulls catch their fish
That God has prepared as their favorite dish?

Let's always thank and praise His name
For the beautiful works He has done.
Remember, we have a race to run,
And the victory has already come.

God's in control!

Copyright ©1996 — Dr. Pattie Pendry

Lord, Teach Me How to Pray

THE SHEPHERD THAT LED MY SHEEP ASTRAY

My sheep are scattered all over the pasture.
Where is the shepherd that they are seeking after?
They are so thirsty with no water to drink.
Many are very hungry; they are falling from faint.

Oh! My poor sheep, they need to be nurtured.
In large numbers, they are falling away.
I need a shepherd that truly cares,
And will show my flock where to stay.

Straight is the way, and narrow is the gate,
And there are many falling aside.
They try to get up and walk, and run,
But they have no place to hide.

Woe unto the pastors that are misleading my sheep.
As they call them and beg for their money
With the sheep being confused and not knowing
what to do,
They take their money and give it all to you.

My sheep, My sheep, come walk with Me,
And let me feed you from My bottle.
Remember, I have taught you to hear My voice,
And a stranger you will not follow.

Come, my sheep and follow Me.
You will never be lost again.
I will take your hand and hold it tight
And walk with you until the end.

Copyright © 1997 —Dr. Pattie Pendry

Poems by Dr. Pattie Pendry

HIS LOVE

His love is wider than the ocean.
His love is deeper than the sea.
He took His cross to Calvary
And died for you and me.

He knows the language of the people
All around the world.
He shed His blood upon the cross
So that we would not be lost.

Reach out to Him, He'll take your hand.
He'll pull you up, and you will stand.
He is the Solid Rock, you know.
And He will teach you how to grow.

His love is taller than the mountain.
His love is deeper than the valley, too.
Won't you please give Jesus a chance
To prove His love to you?

Copyright © 1995 — Dr. Pattie Pendry

Lord, Teach Me How to Pray

LIFE HOLDS THIS MOMENT

You see your neighbor across the street.
Oh, some you may never meet.
But when you see them, give them a smile
And they will see Jesus in your eyes.
  Life holds this moment.

Maybe your kids will begin to cry.
You look outside, there's no air in your tires.
Your car you depend upon to drive.
And suddenly tears swell in your eyes.
You throw up your hands and say, "What must I do?"
Remember, He is there with you.
  Life holds this moment.

Last night you forgot to give your teenage son a hug.
He ran away and started to do drugs.
In your heart you know that you care.
But, oh, that poor boy was in despair.
  Life holds this moment.

Your husband went to the doctor.
The news he heard was bad.
He called you on the telephone.
You could tell in his voice he was sad.
You took the time to listen to what he had to say.

Poems by Dr. Pattie Pendry

You couldn't wait to take his hand and say,
"Honey, you are a special man."
  Life holds this moment.

We never can go back to yesterday.
Tomorrow may never come.
Let's always share the time that we have,
And turn it into fun.
  Life holds this moment.

Copyright © 1995 — Dr. Pattie Pendry

Lord, Teach Me How to Pray

WE MAKE THE DIFFERENCE

In this dark and sinful world,
There is no light to shine.
But we make the difference
Carrying His love, which is so divine.

There are thieves and robbers on every side,
Liars and cheaters, too.
We must be the light for Jesus
And show them what to do.

We must walk in the spirit and talk in the spirit
To be more like Jesus each day.
And to take God's faithful hand
So we can lead each other that way.

Don't get caught up in material things
Or fall into deep, dark sin.
Let your light continue to shine,
And the souls out there you will win.

Copyright © 1997 — Dr. Pattie Pendry

Poems by Dr. Pattie Pendry

HOPE

Look to this day
With hope, joy, peace and love.
Look to tomorrow
With sunshine, brightness
Flowers and dew.
Remember, God is love
And there is always hope.

Copyright © 1995 —Dr. Pattie Pendry

Lord, Teach Me How to Pray

GOD'S CREATION

I like to watch the birds,
Also the butterflies too.
I see the bees come buzzing
That God made for me and you.

The raccoon comes up every day
To get his daily food.
I look at him and begin to pray,
And thank God that He made a way.

And then I see the squirrel so bright,
That doesn't come around at night.
But then I see the fireflies too
That God has made for me and you.

The sun He made to shine by day,
The moon to shine at night.
The stars that look down from above
To show us the creation of love.

So, always remember to worship God,
The Creator from Heaven above
And not the things that He has made.
But worship Him that gives us grace.

Copyright © 1995 — Dr. Pattie Pendry

Poems by Dr. Pattie Pendry

LIFE WITHOUT RAIN

Do flowers bloom without rain?
Does life go on without pain?
What kind of world would it be
If we never experience liberty?

Look at the trees, they stand very tall.
You see the leaves before they fall.
When spring comes, the leaves are green.
The trees still standing as if to sing.

The heart controls the body and soul.
The hurt will come someday.
The pain will come once in a while.
But Jesus is there to stay.

Always remember, the sun will shine
When the dark clouds have rolled away,
The rain has ceased, the flowers have bloomed.
Oh! what a beautiful day!

Copyright © 1997 — Dr. Pattie Pendry

Lord, Teach Me How to Pray

THE HAND

*The Hand of God is with me
Wherever I must go.
He is always there to lead me
And guide me through the door.*

*The Hand of God is with me.
He covers me under His wings.
He is always there to listen
And bless me as I sing.*

*The Hand of God is with me.
He talks to me each night.
He tells me not to worry
Nor let my heart be fright.*

*The Hand of God is with me.
He promised He would always be there.
He reaches out to everyone,
To let them know that He cares.*

*The Hand of God is with me.
He lifts me up higher each day.
I am so glad I know Him
And He taught me the way.*

Copyright © 1996 — Dr Pattie Pendry

Poems by Dr. Pattie Pendry

GOD WILL SEE YOU THROUGH

*Sometimes your heart is breaking
And no one seems to care.
Trouble comes all around you
As your life grows in despair.*

*Suddenly you begin to feel lonely.
You are stricken with great pain.
With no one there to comfort you
Or touch and hold your hand.*

*People began to talk about you
And say things that aren't true.
In your heart you know they are false
And you wonder what to do.*

*Look up and see the rainbow
That God painted in the sky.
See the sun as it began to shine
And know that He is close by.*

*Just remember that He loves you so
As He wipes away your tears.
He will take your hand and hold it high
And make you light as a butterfly.*

God will see you through.

Copyright © 1996 — Dr. Pattie Pendry

Lord, Teach Me How to Pray

THE LONELY TREE

I once was very happy
When I lived in the forest.
There were trees all around me:
Oak, maple, pine, and bark.

The animals would come and play
And make nests in the trees.
The birds would sing and fly all day
and scratch between the leaves.

The birds would find food on the ground
and my branches were green and wide.
The children would run underneath and play.
We all were happy from inside.

Then one day the machines came by
And pushed down all the trees.
All my friends, they went away
And only left their leaves.

God promised us a new Heaven one day
and also a new Earth.
I thank Jesus for being on that tree
So none of us would perish.

But, of course, we have a choice
To make upon our own.

Poems by Dr. Pattie Pendry

Please make the right decision
So you can find your home.

There is going to be a new Heaven one day
and also a new Earth.
I am happy I found my victory
That died upon that lonely tree.

Copyright © 1996 — Dr. Pattie Pendry

Lord, Teach Me How to Pray

GOD IS AWESOME

We see the stars that twinkle at night.
We see the moon so full and bright.
We see the sun so bright and light.
We know that God does everything right.

We also look up into the sky.
We see the birds as they fly by.
We see the rainbow God painted too.
We then look down at His morning dew.

We see the rain, we watch it fall.
We see the trees so green and tall.
We see the grass so green and wet.
We know that God always does His best.

We see the mountains with His highest peak.
We see the valleys that He made so deep.
We see the rivers from shore to shore.
We also know there is even more.

We see the people from around the world.
We see the children, the boys and girls.
We shouldn't see color of their faces.
We should only see their love and heart in places.

Copyright © 1996 — Dr. Pattie Pendry

Poems by Dr. Pattie Pendry

LET'S COME TOGETHER

Why can't we come together
Without bitterness or strife,
To be there for each other
As a man is for his wife?

Why do we see the color
Of a person's skin
When all we need to recognize
Is the heart that is there within?

Why do we hate each other
Because one is black or white?
You see, God made all of us,
And we are precious in His sight.

When a person's skin is red
Or maybe their color is yellow,
Some people began to offend them,
But we need to be there for each other.

You see, God created all of us
From all around the world.
Let's come together and hold hands
So our life will not be in a twirl.

When are we going to reach out for peace
From all our sisters and brothers
And come together within that great love
That God wants us to have for each other?

Copyright © 1997 — Dr. PattiePendry

We hope you have enjoyed reading this book, that you were blessed, and that it will change your life and increase your faith.

If you would like Dr. Pendry to speak at your church, conduct a workshop or seminar, or would like to receive any additional information, please write or call:

> International for Jesus Ministries
> P.O. Box 13007
> Raleigh, NC 27605
>
> (919) 755-1547
> (919) 876-7228

New books soon to come:
> *My Romance With Jesus*
> *Benny the Clown*

Salvation tracts available now:
> *When is your birthday?*
> *Would you like free gifts?*